T0016887

CELEBRATING
ST. PATRICK'S DAY

CELEBRATING

ST. PATRICK'S DAY

History, Traditions, and Activities
A HOLIDAY BOOK FOR KIDS

John O'Brien, Jr.

Illustrations by Ellen Shi

ROCKRIDGE
PRESS

Interior and Cover Designer: Antonio Valverde and Jane Archer
Art Producer: Hannah Dickerson
Editor: Garth Haller, Lauren Moore and Alyson Penn
Production Editor: Ashley Polikoff
Illustrations © 2020 Ellen Shi

ISBN: Hardcover 978-1-63878-840-9 | Paperback 978-1-64739-687-9 | eBook 978-1-64739-422-6
R0

To the storytellers, singers, and
songwriters across the world, poets and
teachers all, who carry on the bardic
tradition and share our rich Irish heritage
with passion, fun, and love. Thank you!

CONTENTS

WHAT IS ST. PATRICK'S DAY?

St. Patrick's Day is a day of celebration in honor of one of three official church patron saints of Ireland. Called the apostle of Ireland, Patrick was a holy man who taught Christianity to the Irish people sometime during the fifth century, more than 1,500 years ago. All around the world, on March 17 or the weekend nearest to it, people honor St. Patrick and observe St. Patrick's Day. For many, the day is a religious occasion, but it is also a celebration of Irish culture and people in general.

Every year, communities across the globe hold St. Patrick's Day parades. These special events are big reunions of family and friends where people also create new memories and friendships.

Even though Ireland is smaller than the state of Ohio, Irish people now live all over the world. They are known as the Irish **diaspora**, an old word similar in meaning to "scattered" that refers to people who live far from their original homeland. No matter where Irish people have settled, they celebrate St. Patrick's Day in remembrance of their families and homes in Ireland.

More than 450 churches in the United States are named for St. Patrick.

HISTORY AND FOLKLORE

IRISH WORDS AND FOLKTALES

Today, English is the second official language of Ireland and is used for most business in the country. Ireland's first official language has always been Irish, however, and for many centuries it was the primary language. In Ireland, people call that language Irish, but in the United States, it is sometimes called "Irish Gaelic." ("Gaelic" is the English word for *Gaeilge*, which means "Irish" in the Irish language.) To this day, many public signs in Ireland are posted in both Irish and English. Of the 2 million people who speak Irish today, more than 1.7 million live in Ireland. This is partly because learning the Irish language is required in public schools in Ireland.

Because the Irish language is such an important part of the culture of Ireland, many people use Irish words and phrases as part of celebrating St. Patrick's

Day. For example, the Irish phrase for "St. Patrick's Day" is *Lá Fhéile Pádraig* (pronounced *Law Ale-yeh Pawd-rig*), which literally translates to "the Feast of St. Patrick" or "the Day of the Festival of St. Patrick."

An Irish storyteller is called a bard or, in Irish, a *seanachie* (pronounced *shawn-neck-key*). Irish people love Irish folklore—the old songs and stories that make up the culture—because they not only entertain, but

also help people remember the people and places their parents told them about when they were little. These stories tell the history of Ireland and of their families, and are passed from generation to generation. Similarly, the history of St. Patrick's Day is linked closely to rich, old traditions of Irish storytelling, especially legends and folktales.

According to one of the famous old Irish folktales, St. Patrick drove the snakes out of Ireland. This tale is similar to a **parable**, a made-up or fictional story that teaches a lesson or explains an idea, rather than a true story based on actual facts and events. For example, the story includes snakes, even though Ireland was probably far too cold for snakes to survive. In many tales, including this one, snakes symbolize bad or mean things. According to the story, when St. Patrick introduced Ireland to Christianity, he drove away evil, symbolized by the snakes.

PATRICK'S BIG STICK AND TALL HAT

St. Patrick lived such a long time ago that we have no pictures of him. Our ideas about what he looked like came from stories written much later, many of which are folklore or legends.

Because the ground in Ireland is often rocky, St. Patrick supposedly carried a special walking stick called a **crozier**. Patrick was also said to wear a distinctive tall hat called a **mitre**. The crozier and mitre are symbols of standing in the church.

Because Patrick was a holy man who traveled throughout Ireland, many Irish folktales and religious stories are about his walking stick. One legend says the top of the walking stick curled around in a circle instead of ending in a cross. Local folklore said Jesus gave the walking stick to a hermit to hold until St. Patrick arrived, which is why the stick came to be called the **Bachal Isu**, or the Staff of Jesus. According to another legend, one day when Patrick was preaching, he placed his wooden walking stick in the ground, and by the time he was ready to leave, the stick had taken root and become a living tree.

ST. PATRICK'S NICKNAME

We often shorten names into nicknames. Susan becomes Susie. Jennifer can become Jen. Patricia can become Pat or Patty. James becomes Jim or Jimmy. Joseph becomes Joe or Joey. And Patrick gets shortened to Paddy. When we shorten St. Patrick, we call him St. Paddy (not St. Patty!).

ARE A SHAMROCK AND A CLOVER THE SAME THING?

The shamrock is a symbol of Ireland. The word "shamrock" comes from an old Irish word, *seamróg* (pronounced *sham-rogue*), for all types of clover plants. Many people think shamrocks and clovers are the same plant, but they are not. A clover can have three or four leaves, and the shamrock is a type of clover that has three leaves. The three-leaf shamrock and four-leaf clover are symbols with different meanings.

St. Patrick was clever. He used the shamrock to explain how the religion of Christianity works. The three-leaf shamrock is a symbol for the Holy Trinity in Christianity. A trinity is a group of three things, such as the three lines that form a triangle or the three leaves of a shamrock. St. Patrick used the shamrock to show how the three parts of the Christian god that make up the Holy Trinity—the Father (God), the Son (Jesus), and the Holy Spirit—are working together as one. In stories, the leaves of a four-leaf clover represent faith, hope, love, and luck.

Many people think of the four-leaf clover as lucky, but Irish people consider the three-leaf shamrock to be the lucky version of the clover. On St. Patrick's Day, shamrocks decorate hats, cheeks, floats, pins, and much more.

Ireland's shortest St. Patrick's Day parade, held in the village of Dripsey, spans only 25 yards!

WHAT IS A LEPRECHAUN?

A **leprechaun** is
a kind of fairy
from Irish folklore,
but not all fairies
are leprechauns.
Mischievous elves,
leprechauns are
often shoemakers
who fix other

leprechauns' shoes and believe someone is trying to
steal their gold. When someone is daydreaming or
acting a bit unusual, people say they are "away with
the fairies."

Called "leps" or "wee folk" for short—because they
are small and can hide almost anywhere—leprechauns
are cranky souls. Legend has it that wearing green
makes a person invisible to leprechauns, which is
important because leps will pinch you if they see you!
Some say leps hide their gold at the end of a rainbow.
Can you get there fast enough to grab it before the
rainbow disappears?

PREPARING FOR ST. PATRICK'S DAY

Preparing for St. Patrick's Day is often as much fun as the holiday itself. Families put on Irish music and sing while they decorate their homes with crafts and ornaments such as leprechauns, fairy folk, rainbows, pots of gold, shamrocks, Irish flags, and green carnations. Adults make sure their kitchens are full of Irish treats to enjoy.

In case the wee folk come to see how they are dec-
orating, they also wear lots of green. Another way
to make sure leprechauns can't make mischief on
St. Patrick's Day is to catch them in a leprechaun trap.
(Check out the Culture Corner, page 32, to learn how
to make one yourself!)

Should the St. Patrick's Day color
change to blue? In 1783, the Order of
St. Patrick's color was a light blue
named "St. Patrick's Blue."

WHAT TO WEAR

It's St. Patrick's Day, so of course people wear green!

Will it be warm or cold that day? If it's cold, they bundle up with an Irish sweater and a **tam o' shanter**, an Irish hat that looks like a flat, round bonnet or beret. Other great choices are green shirts, socks, hats, gloves, jackets, and dresses. Ribbons and flags in the colors of the Irish flag are all great choices, too.

No matter what, the most important thing to wear all day is a smile!

HOW TO CELEBRATE

Many people who have Irish heritage were born in the United States, but their parents, grandparents, or even great-grandparents were born in Ireland and immigrated here. Their families in Ireland may go back to the time of St. Patrick during the fifth century, or even earlier!

You also don't have to be of Irish heritage to celebrate St. Patrick's Day. Everyone can participate in the fun. Whether you are attending a parade, enjoying an Irish festival, or watching Irish dancers soar and fly, all are welcome. Everyone is Irish on St. Patrick's Day!

REMEMBERING ST. PATRICK

The Irish have observed St. Patrick's Day as a religious holiday for more than 1,000 years. Many people begin the day by attending church to remember how St. Patrick brought Christianity to Ireland, then have a quick lunch with family or friends before going to the parade. The day is filled with traditions shared by the entire family, from the youngest children to their parents and grandparents.

ST. PATRICK'S DAY PARADES

Watching the parade, waving to marchers, and seeing family and friends make the day festive and fun. High school bands, floats, dancers, and different groups march together, competing with other groups to win first place for artwork, creativity, and fun. At the St. Patrick's Day Parade in Cleveland, Ohio, special shamrock pins engraved with the year are sold. Celebrators love a good luck charm they can show off proudly!

Even if it is cold, everyone bundles up to get nice and warm to go to the parade. They find a great spot to see all the marchers, floats, and bands, and while they wait, they can practice new Irish words. If no St. Patrick's Day parade is nearby, organize one of your own on your street or in your neighborhood. Invite family, friends, and neighbors to help. It's a great way to meet new people in your community.

The Irish alphabet has only 18 letters.

VISITING WITH FAMILY

After the parade and dinner, family and friends gather together, sharing songs, stories, memories, and lots of laughter. Then the music starts. If people are just playing instruments casually and listening, it is called a *sessiún* (pronounced *sesh-shune),* or a jam session. A social gathering with Irish folk music and dancing is called a *cèilidh* or *céili* (pronounced kay-lee) for short. It is fun to learn dances from all over Ireland and share them at the *céili.*

TREASURE HUNTS

Legend says a pot of gold is a treasure that can be found at the end of each rainbow. But rainbows are rare, so for St. Patrick's Day, people organize treasure hunts on their own. Brothers, sisters, aunts and uncles, friends, and babysitters can all help plan a fun event for the whole neighborhood. They can use many different items: treasure chests made of small pails or flowerpots painted black; gold-covered coins or candy; green lollipops, cookies, and cupcakes; or even a few shamrock seeds to grow at home in the days leading up to St. Patrick's Day. Once they have gathered all their treasures, parents and grandparents can hide them in the yard or around the house, and the children can hunt for them!

AROUND THE WORLD

St. Patrick's Day is a national public holiday in Ireland, but people celebrate the holiday all over the world, especially in the United States, which has more than 100 St. Patrick's Day celebrations every year. American cities including Boston, New York

City, Philadelphia, and Savannah have held St. Patrick's Day parades since the 18th and early 19th centuries.

In Chicago, people take the fun a step further. Every St. Patrick's Day, workers dye the Chicago River green. The tint lasts only about half a day, but the green river has become a cherished tradition for people celebrating St. Patrick's Day in the city for more than 50 years!

In many cities in Ireland, the United States, and other countries around the world, people go well beyond the parade to celebrate their rich Irish heritage on St. Patrick's Day.

Dublin, Ireland's largest city, holds a three-day cultural festival that includes a parade, live music, dance, festive foods, pipe bands, and sports.

Tourists expecting a beach paradise are surprised to find that the tropical island of Montserrat is also known as the "Emerald Isle of the Caribbean." First settled by the Irish in the 1600s, this small, vibrant island not only declares St. Patrick's Day an official national holiday, but it also has a shamrock for its passport stamp. Locals and visitors alike flock there for weeklong St. Patrick's Day festivities highlighting local Caribbean culture and their Irish heritage. In addition to parades featuring masked street dancers, vibrant costumes, and steel drum bands, residents take part in the Freedom Run, which celebrates the freedom of both African enslaved people and Irish indentured servants.

In Savannah, Georgia, the St. Patrick's Day festivities go on for several days and include food and music festivals, as well as a parade. The water in the famous Forsyth Park Fountain is also dyed green for the occasion.

The Irish community in Brussels, Belgium, celebrates St. Patrick's Day throughout the Parc du Cinquantenaire ("Park of the 50th Anniversary") and hosts a sports tournament in which **Gaelic football**, **hurling**, and **camogie** are played. Gaelic football is similar to soccer, but players are allowed to use their hands. Hurling, the national sport of Ireland, is like a combination of the American sports field hockey and lacrosse. Players use a hurl, a wooden stick that resembles a hockey stick, to hit the ball to one another while racing up and down a grassy field. The ball is in the air most of the time, and players score points when they hit the ball between the goal posts. Camogie is the women's version of hurling.

In Ise, Japan, marchers gather at the Ise Shrine to kick off St. Patrick's Day. When the parade begins, the flags of Japan and Ireland fly side by side, and Japanese residents do jigs, play bagpipes, and dress up like leprechauns and St. Patrick. Hungry marchers continue to celebrate at an oyster festival.

St. Patrick's Day has even been celebrated in outer space—twice. While she was in orbit at the International Space Station in 2011, astronaut Cady Coleman played a 100-year-old flute owned by Irish traditional music legend Matt Molloy, a member of the famous Irish band The Chieftains. The Chieftains loved Cady's playing so much, they put her music on one of their albums. In 2013, astronaut Chris Hadfield sent home pictures of beautiful Ireland at night from the International Space Station.

Did you know 14 dog breeds are native to Ireland? The largest dog—in the world, not just Ireland—is the Irish wolfhound. The smallest Irish dog is the Glen of Imaal terrier.

THE CITY OF DUBLIN

Located on the eastern side of the island, Dublin is the capital of Ireland and its largest city. The name "Dublin" means "black water." In honor of Ireland's capital, more than a dozen communities in the United States are also called Dublin.

CULTURE CORNER

S t. Patrick's Day is a special occasion for many exciting games and other activities, crafts, and recipes.

PARADE BINGO GAME

This is a fun way to compete against your family and friends at your local St. Patrick's Day parade or festival.

MATERIALS

A Parade Bingo card similar to the one that appears below

A pen, pencil, or marker

1. Create your own Parade Bingo cards or ask your parents to make copies of the sample one pictured here. The cards should contain rows of boxes, with each box containing a symbol or decoration related to Ireland and St. Patrick's Day. If you're not sure what to put on your card, flip through this book to get ideas.

2. Find a good spot to watch the parade marchers.

3. When you see an item that appears on your card, shout the name of it out and mark off the matching square on your card.

4. The first person to get five in a row wins.

RAINBOW SHAKERS/ NOISEMAKERS

You can use rainbow shakers to play music or make noise at St. Patrick's Day parades. They are also a great souvenir to keep for other special events. If you need help, ask a parent or another adult.

MATERIALS

Glue or tape

Black construction paper

Paper towel rolls

Scissors

Colored construction paper (ideally in all the colors of the rainbow—red, orange, yellow, green, blue, and purple)

Uncooked rice, marbles, or small pebbles

Cotton balls

Small gold-colored bells, gold tinsel, gold glitter, gold stickers, or other gold decorations

1. Glue or tape a piece of black construction paper across one end of the paper towel roll so the hole is completely blocked off.

2. Cut the black and the colored construction paper into ½-inch-wide strips.

3. Starting at the end that is blocked off, wrap a black strip around the roll, and glue or tape it into place. The black strip represents the pot of gold.

4. Wrap a strip of colored paper right next to the black strip, and glue or tape it into place. Repeat with the next color strip until you have a full rainbow. To create a typical rainbow effect, place the color strips in this order: red, orange, yellow, green, blue, and purple. But you can also use any order you like.

5. Place the rice, marbles, or pebbles inside the roll. Leave enough space so the rice or pebbles will make noise when you shake the roll.

6. At the top of the roll, glue or tape another piece of black paper across the end so the hole is completely blocked off.

7. Glue or tape cotton balls at the top of the roll to represent clouds at the other end of the rainbow.

8. Glue or tape the gold decorations between the black and first colored strip to look like the pot is filled with gold.

9. Repeat steps 1 to 8 to make as many shakers as you want.

GREEN SCAVENGER HUNT

On St. Patrick's Day, we wear green. But you can find plenty of other green things if you look closely enough! Gather your family, friends, or classmates and see how many green things you can find on this list:

FIND SOMETHING GREEN THAT ...

1. You can eat
2. You can wear
3. You can write with
4. You can play with
5. Has writing or words on it
6. Is hard
7. Is soft
8. Is on a wall
9. Is outside
10. Is something that grows

LEPRECHAUN TRAP

Legend says that leprechauns can't resist a treat, so you can use sweets to lure and catch them in a leprechaun trap. When they follow the trail of sweets to the big pile, you can knock the stick down to trap them under the hat or upside-down pot of gold!

MATERIALS

Green construction paper

Colored stickers, shamrocks, Irish flags, or other green or Irish decorations

Small sweet treats, such as candy or sugary cereal

A *shillelagh*, which is a walking stick made from a branch of a blackthorn tree, or a wooden stick from the yard

A green hat or a small black pot that looks like a pot of gold

1. Decorate a piece of green construction paper with stickers, shamrocks, Irish flags, or other items.

2. Scatter a pile of the treats on the paper.

3. Use the stick to prop up the green hat or upside-down pot of gold over the pile of sweets, similar to an umbrella.

4. Make a trail of even more sweets leading to the pile under the hat or pot of gold.

IRISH FLAG OR SHAMROCK COOKIES

Decorate cookies with the colors of the Irish flag, shape them to look like a shamrock, or both.

INGREDIENTS

½ cup (1 stick) unsalted butter, at room temperature, plus more for greasing

1 (3-ounce) package instant pistachio pudding mix

1⅓ cups cookie baking mix

1 large egg

1 tablespoon white sugar

All-purpose white flour, for dusting

Cookie cutters (shamrock, rectangle, or both)

White cookie-decorating icing

Green food coloring

Orange food coloring (only needed for Irish flag cookies)

1. Preheat the oven to 350°F. Lightly grease a baking sheet.

2. In a large bowl, combine the butter and pudding mix. Add the baking mix, egg, and sugar and mix well.

3. On a lightly floured surface, roll out the dough to a ⅜-inch thickness and cut into shamrock or rectangular shapes. Transfer the cookies to the prepared baking sheet.

4. Bake for 9 to 10 minutes, or until lightly browned on the edges. Let the cookies cool on a wire rack.

5. To make shamrock cookies, use the green food coloring to tint the icing to your desired shade of green. To make Irish flag cookies, divide the icing equally among three bowls. Tint one bowl of icing with green food coloring and another with orange food coloring.

6. Spread green icing on the shamrock cookies, or green, white, and orange icing on the Irish flag cookies.

SHAMROCK SHAKES

A favorite St. Patrick's Day treat is a milkshake dyed green. *Note*: Ask an adult to help with this recipe, especially when using the blender!

INGREDIENTS (MAKES 1)

2 scoops vanilla ice cream (or any flavor you love)

1 cup whole milk

1 tablespoon mint extract (adjust to taste preferences)

Green food coloring

1 tablespoon whipped cream

Green sprinkles

Maraschino cherries

Optional: chocolate chips, green candy, chocolate syrup, or other toppings

1. In a blender, mix the ice cream, milk, and mint extract on high. Add a bit of the food coloring and continue mixing. Repeat as needed to your desired shade of green.

2. Pour the shake into a clear glass.

3. Top with whipped cream, green sprinkles, a cherry, and any other treats.

LEARN TO SAY IT!

Here are a few Irish phrases and words to say during St. Patrick's Day:

Lá Fhéile Pádraig
Law Ale-yeh Pawd-rig

ST. PATRICK'S DAY or
THE FEAST OF ST. PATRICK

Seamróg
sham-rogue

ALL CLOVER PLANTS,
INCLUDING THE SHAMROCK

Cèilidh or céili
kay-lee

A SOCIAL GATHERING WITH
IRISH FOLK MUSIC AND DANCING

Sessiún
sesh-shune

JAM SESSION

Seanachie
shawn-neck-key

IRISH STORYTELLER

GLOSSARY

Bachal Isu: The Staff of Jesus, the special walking stick (also called a *crozier*) that was supposedly later given to St. Patrick

camogie: The women's version of the sport of hurling

cèilidh: A social gathering that typically involves Irish folk music and dancing, also called a *céili*

crozier: A special walking stick carried by St. Patrick

diaspora: People who live far from their original homeland

Dublin: The Irish word for "black water" and the name of the capital city of Ireland and several communities in the United States

Gaelic football: A sport similar to soccer in which players are allowed to use their hands

hurling: The national sport of Ireland, similar to the US sports field hockey and lacrosse

leprechaun: A small, mischievous green-clad fairy of Irish legend, often a shoemaker, who is always hiding, protecting, or searching for his pot of gold

mitre: A distinctive tall hat worn by St. Patrick

parable: A made-up or fictional story told to teach a lesson, often as part of a religion

seamróg: The old Irish word for all clover plants, including the shamrock.

seanachie: The Irish word for "storyteller"; also called a *bard* in Ireland

sessiún: A jam session gathering of musicians playing instruments and listening

shillelagh: A walking stick made from a branch of a blackthorn tree

St. Patrick: One of the three official church patron saints of Ireland; he taught Christianity to the people of Ireland

tam o' shanter: A traditional Irish cap that looks like a flat, round bonnet or beret

RESOURCES

WEBSITES

Irish Central: IrishCentral.com

National Geographic Kids: Kids.National
Geographic.com/explore/celebrations
/st-patricks-day

Ohio Irish American News: OhioIANews.com

St. Patrick's Day Activities: Education.com
/activity/st-patricks-day

BOOKS (FICTION)

Have You Seen My Pot of Gold? (printable mini book).
New York: Scholastic.

Wallace, Adam, and Andy Elkerton. *How to Catch
a Leprechaun*. Naperville, IN: Sourcebooks
Wonderland, 2016.

Wojciechowski, Susan, and Tom Curry. *A Fine
St. Patrick's Day*. Decorah, IL: Dragonfly Books, 2008.

ABOUT THE AUTHOR

First-generation Irish American **John O'Brien, Jr.,** is the author of five books; an award-winning poet; a founder of the Cleveland Irish Cultural Festival, where he served as deputy director for 36 years; and the founder, publisher, and editor of the *Ohio Irish American News*. The *OhioIANews* is a monthly newsmagazine featuring news, events, and the Irish movers, shakers, and music makers, aimed at the 1.6 million Ohioans of Irish descent. You can find the *OhioIANews* on Facebook, Twitter, and Instagram. For regular updates, subscribe to the monthly eBulletin on the *OhioIANews* website and check out the *Songs, Stories & Shenanigans* podcast, hosted twice a month on WHKRadio.com and OhioIANews.com.

ABOUT THE ILLUSTRATOR

 As a child, **Ellen Shi** was often found with her nose between the pages of a book.

She went on to get her BFA in illustration from Rhode Island School of Design and works as a designer in California and a freelance children's book illustrator. She thinks children's books are her calling since the excitement of slapping down a color and the response when sharing illustration makes her feel like she's on top of the world. She is inspired by everyday life, nature, and color, and you can find her listening to audiobooks, binge-watching movies, or enjoying nature.